# PEGGY'S SCRAPB

G000146726

## Monthly Weather Sa
## by Peggy Cole

First Published by LUCAS BOOKS 2004
ISBN 1903797-43-8

## Copyright Peggy Cole 2004

Printed in the UK by Winsor Clarke Brackenbury Limited

# JANUARY

If New Year's Day happens on a Saturday, the Winter will be mean and the Summer hot

A Summerish January, a Winterish Spring

If on St. Vincent's day the sky is clear, More wine than water will crown the year

Sound travelling far and wide, A stormy day betide

When oak trees bend with snow in January, good crops may be expected

If the birds begin to sing in January, frosts are on the way

January warm - let the Lord have mercy

As the days lengthen, So does the cold strengthen

A favourable January brings a good year

Hoar frost and no snow is hurtful to fields, trees and grain

In January, if the sun appear, March and April will pay full dear

The severest winters are those which begin about 6 January having been preceded by a mild December

If the month of January is like a gentleman as he begins, so he goes on
13 January *(St Hilary)* the coldest day of the year

January blossoms fill no man's cellar

He who would fill his pouch with groats, In January must sow his oats

If the first snow falls on moist soft earth it indicates a small harvest but if on hard frozen soil then there will be a good harvest

If there is no snow before January there will be more in March and April
If on 12th January the sun shines, it foreshows much wind

The first three days in January rule the coming three months

January commits the fault and May bears the blame

If birds whistle in January, frost will follow

Hail brings frost in the tail

The frost hurts no weeds

If there's Spring in Winter and Winter in Spring, The year won't be good for anything

A white frost never lasts more than three days. A long frost is a black frost

If the south wind blow on St Vincent's day, T'will scare the frost of March away

Fog in January brings a wet Spring

Much rain in January, no blessing to the fruit

The last twelve days of January ride the weather for the whole year

# FEBRUARY

On Candlemas Day, a good goose will lay, But on St Valentine's Day, any goose will lay

A February spring is not worth a pin

After Candlemas Day, the frost will be more keen
If the sun then shines bright,
than before it has been
If Candlemas Day be dry and fair,
There'll be two Winters in the year
On St Valentine's Day, set the Hopper by Mind
*(All planting should be under serious consideration by then)*

After a wet year, a cold one

All the months of the year curse a fair February

Winter's back breaks about the middle of February

There is always one fine week in February

St Matthie *(24 February)* sends sap into the tree St Matthias sows both leaf and grass

When gnats dance in February, the Husbandman becomes a Beggar

For this was on St Valentine's Day, when every fowl cometh to choose her mate

If gnats hum on the last of February, they will be dumb for the whole of March
If in February there be no rain, 'Tis neither good for hay nor grain

Fogs in February mean frost in May

St Matthew breaks the ice, if he finds none, he will make it

Sow cabbage when February moon is old

When a cow turns her tail to the wind it means rain

Warm February bad hay crop, Cold February, good hay crop

When the cat in February lies in the sun, she will creep behind the stove in March

For every thunder with rain in February, there will be a cold spell in May

Violent north winds in February herald a fertile year

When drops hang on the fence on 2 February icicles will hang there on 25 March

The night of St Peter *(22 February)* shows what weather we shall have for the next forty days

When the north wind does not blow in February, it will surely come in March

Whenever the bees get about in February, we are certain to get wind and rain next day

11 February the Rooks start to build, 12th February the toad makes a noise and on 17 February the bee begins to appear

If Candlemas Day be gay and bright Winter will have another flight, But if Candlemas Day brings clouds and rain, Winter has gone, and won't come again.
If Candlemas Day *(February 2nd)* be fine and clear corn and fruits will be dear

## MARCH

March buys Winter's cloak and sells it in three days

A dry and cold March never begs its bread

On the first of March the crows begin to search

March comes in with an adder's head and goes out with a peacock's tail

When it thunders in March it brings sorrow

When elm leaves are as big as a shillin', plant kidney beans if to plant `em you're willin'. When elm leaves are as big as a penny, you must plant kidney beans if you're to have any

In the beginning or the end, March its gifts will send

Upon St David's day, put oats and barley in the clay

St Patrick's Day, the warm side of a stone turns up and the broad back goose begins to lay

When round the moon there is a burgh, the weather will be cold and rough

March dry, good rye, March wet, good wheat

When the wind's in the south it blows bait in the fish's mouth

March wind flowers so frail and pure keep all infection from your door

A peck of March dust and a shower in May, make the corn green and the fields gay

March dust on an apple leaf brings all kinds of fruit to grief

Beware the blackthorn winter

For every frost in March, there'll be a frost in May

As many Misties in March As many Frosties in May

Cold March, wet April and hot May will make the fruit year they say

Spit on a frog's head in March and the frog will carry your cough away

If March come in like a lion, it goes out like a lamb

A late spring never deceives

A wet March makes a sad Harvest

A bushel of March dust is a thing worth the ransom of a king, Dust in March brings grass and foliage

Better be bitten by a snake than to feel the sun in March

When March has April weather, April will have March weather

When the blackthorn blossoms white Sow the barley day and night.

So many fogs in March
So many Frost in May

A dry March never begs it bread

If sheep go to shade in March, they go to shelter in June

## APRIL

Rain and sunshine both together

April moist and warm makes the farmer sing like a nightingale

April and May are the keys to the year

April and May between them make bread for all the day

Thunderstorm in April is the end of the hoarfrost

If the first three days in April be foggy, Rain in June will make the lanes boggy

Plant your 'taters when you will They won't come up before April

If it thunders on all fools day It brings a good crop of corn and hay

'Tis always cold when the blackthorn is in bloom. The blossom generally appears in March

When on Saint George's rye will hide a cow, a good harvest may be expected

At Saint George's the meadow turns to hay

An April flood carries away the frog and his brood

April snow breeds grass

Fogs in April foretell a failure of the wheat crop next year

After warm April and October, a warm year next

When April blows his horn, it's good for hay and corn

If a rainbow stretch from north to east a spell of dry weather will follow.
If it stretch from east to west, gales are coming

When the thrush sings at sunset a fair day will follow

When the cuckoo comes to the bare thorn, sell your cow and buy your corn
But when she comes to the full bit, sell your corn and buy your sheep

If the sun shines of Easter Day, it shines on Whit Sunday likewise

Early blossoms indicate a bad fruit year

A cold April brings both bread and wine

Whatever March does not want, April brings along

If there's Spring in Winter and Winter in Spring The year won't be good for anything

April showers bring summer flowers

April with both sunshine and showers Brings out all the wild flowers

April cold and wet fills both barn and barr

## MAY

The later the blackthorn in bloom after the first of May, the better the rye and harvest

Two moons in May, no fruit or hay

A hot May makes for a fat churchyard.

No weather is ill if the wind be still

Water in May is bread all the year

Cold May good for corn and rain in May makes plenty of hay

March winds and April showers bring forth May flowers

Don't cast a clout 'til May is out *[reference to the Mayflower]*

April and May are the keys to the year
May kittens never make good cats. May chicks never grow to full size

Shear your sheep in May and you'll shear them all the way

A dry May and a dripping June bring all things in tune

If cocks in the afternoon do crow, some change is at hand for weal or woe

From your apple trees keep witches away or they'll blight the bloom on St Dunstan's day

Heat in May gives strength to the whole year

May 9th to 14th Buchan's third cold period
*[In Europe these days are known as the festivals of the ice men]*

Easterly winds on 19th to 21st May indicate a dry summer

Flowers in May, fine cocks of hay

When May is dry the following September is apt to be wet

The more thunder in May, the less in August and September

For an east wind of May 'tis your duty to pray

In the middle of May comes the tail of the winter

A swarm of bees in May is worth a load of hay A swarm of bees in June is worth a silver spoon But a swarm of bees in July isn't worth a fly

What grows in May should be eaten in May

If the weather be fine on the last of May, the mowers may look for abundance of hay

If the ash before the oak, then we'll surely get a soak If the oak before the ash, then we'll only get a splash

A wet May makes a long-tailed hay

A cold May and a windy barn filleth up finely

A misty May and a hot June

Bring cheap meal and harvest soon

It is May, it is May, and we bless the day For now the winter is quite away

A dry May portends a wholesome summer

If the apple tree blooms in May, You can eat apple dumplings every day

May never goes out without a wheat ear

Water in May brings bread through all the year

A leaky May and a dry June, Keep a poor man's head in abundance

A rainy May brings plenty of corn and hay

A cold May enriches no-one

When you hear the cuckoo shout Tis time to plant your 'tattlers' out

# JUNE

When the wind is in the North the skillful fisher goes not forth
When the wind is in the South it blows the bait in the fish's mouth
When the wind is in the East they won't bite in the least
But when the wind is in the West the fish bite best

Mist in May and heat in June makes the harvest ripen soon

June damp and warm does the farmer no harm

In April the cuckoo shows his bill
In May he sings both night and day
In June he altereth his tune
In July away he'll fly In August go he must

June, if sunny, brings harvest early

Garlic in June is worth a silver spoon
Cut your thistles before St John, you will have two instead of one
Cut'em in June they'll come again soon
Cut'em in July they may die
Cut'em in August and die they must

A dripping June brings all things in tune

Rain on St Barnabas's Day *(llth)* is good for grapes

A dry May and a leaking June makes the farmer whistle a tune

June 21st summer begins; June 24th Midsummer Day

When the dogwood flower appear Frost will not again be here

If it rains on Midsummer Eve *(23rd)* the filberts will be spoiled

If a cuckoo sings after St John's Day *(24th)* the harvest will be late

An idle man expects potatoes to grow by his fireside
A load of hay in June is worth two in July

If St John's wort is gathered on the eve of St John's Day and hung up near the door or window, it will act as a protection against evil spirits and any dangers that may come with thunder

A wet June makes a dry September, Calm weather in June, Sets corn in tune

Before St John's Day we pray for rain, after that we get it anyhow

When the wind goes to the west early in June, expect wet weather 'til the end of August

A mild, wet winter always follows an unproductive summer

If the cuckoo does not cease singing at midsummer, corn will be dear

A cold and wet June spoils the rest of the year

If St Vitus Day be rainy weather It will rain for thirty days together
On St Barnabas' put the scythe to the grass

Seagull, seagull, sit on the sand,
It's never good weather while you're on the land

# JULY

If the first July be rainy weather
Twill rain more or less four weeks together

Dog days bright and clear, indicate a happy year
But when accompanied by rain
For better times are hopes in vain

Dog day begin. If the dog day be clear, twill be fine all the year

He who bathes in May, will soon be laid in clay.
He who bathes in June, will sing a merry tune.
He who bathes in July will dance like a fly.

If St Margaret *(20 July)* brings the first pear, pears will abound for the rest of the year

The rose is said to begin to fade on St Mary Magdalene's Day *(22 July)*

It is customary to start eating oysters on St James' Day *(25 July)*

When the moon is at the full, mushrooms you may freely pull. But when the moon is on the wane, wait before you pluck again

A dry summer never begs its bread

St Swithin's Day if thou dost rain, for forty days it will remain.
St Swithin's Day if thou be fair, for forty days will rain nae mair.

At St Vincent *(19 July)* the rain ceases and the wind comes

When the sun enters Leo, the greatest heat will then arise

Much thunder in July injures wheat and barley

Swallows high, staying dry,
Swallows low, wet `twill blow
A shower of rain in July, when the corn begins to fill,
Is worth a plough of oxen and all belongs there till

An English summer - three fine days and a thunderstorm

When ant hills are unusually high in July,
the coming winter will be hard and long

July wears sweet peas twined amid her hair,
And in her harvest robe red poppies flare

Ne'er trust a July sky

The English weather ends in July and begins in August

Saint Swithin is christening the apples

The greater the haze, the more settled the weather
A cool summer and a light weight in the bushel

Whatever July and August do not boil, September cannot fry

As the days begin to shorten the heat begins to scorch 'em

All the tears that Saint Swithin can cry,
Saint Bartholomew's dusty mantle wipes dry

A swarm of bees in July is not worth a butterfly

## AUGUST

Lammas Day *(1 August)*, the ancient feast of thanksgiving for the fruit of the corn

After Lammas, corn ripens as much by night as by day

11 August Dog day ends

A rainy August makes a hard bread crust

If the moon show a silver shield, be not afraid to reap your field.
But if she rises haloed round, soon we'll tread on deluged ground

When snails climb up the stalks of grass, wet weather is at hand
When the hen doth moult before the cock, the winter will be as hard as rock.
But if the cock moult before the hen, the winter will not wet your shoe's seam

If a sheep feed uphill in the morning, it is a sign of fine weather

August ripens, September gathers in
August bears the burden, September the fruit

So many August fogs, so many winter mists

On St Mary's Day *(15 August)* sunshine brings much and good wine
'Tis not the husbandman but the good weather that makes the corn grow

Heavy dew at night, next day bright,
Hot day, dewless night, rain in sight

As St Bartholomew's Day *(24 August)*, so the whole autumn

If Bartholomew's Day be fair and clear
Then hope of a prosperous autumn this year

Tender handed touch a nettle and it stings you for your pains
Grasp it like a man of mettle and it soft as milk remains

When a cow tries to scratch it's ear, it means a shower is very near
When it thumps it's ribs with it's tail, look out for thunder, lightning and hail

Dry August and warm, doth harvest no harm. Forgotten month past, do mow at last

A fog in August indicates a severe winter and plenty of snow

If a Heron *(Harnser)* or a Bittern flies low, the air is becoming charged with
water vapour

A rainbow at morn, put your hook in the corn.
A rainbow at eve, put your head in the sheave
If swallows fly high, the weather will be warm

## SEPTEMBER

Fair on 1 September, fair for the month

Warm September brings the fruit
Sportsmen then begin to shoot

Thunder in September indicates a good crop of grain and fruit for next year

Dry, mild September will make cellars full of good ale

Many Haw, many sloes, many cold toes

September dries up wells or breaks down bridges

As on the eighth of September, so for the next four weeks

September blow soft 'til the fruits are in the loft

A good nut year is a good corn year
There are generally three consecutive windy days about the middle of
September, which have been called the windy days of barley harvest

The devil goes nutting on Holy-rood Day *(14 September)*

If on 19 September there is a storm from the south,
a mild winter may be expected

If the storms in September clear off warm
All the storms of the following winter will be warm

A quiet week before the Autumn Equinox *(21 September)* and after the
temperature will continue higher than usual into winter

St Matthew *(21 September)* brings on the cold dew

St Matthew shuts up the bees

So many days old the moon is on Michaelmas day, so many floods after

On Michaelmas day, the devil puts his foot on the blackberries

If rain be coming, geese always gaggle on the pond

If acorns abound in September, Snow will be deep in December

A blue and white sky, never four and twenty hours dry

If St Michael bring thunder, rough weather will follow

Onion skin very thin,
Mild winter coming in.
Onion skin thick and tough
Coming winter cold and rough.

If the ice is strong enough to bear a man before Michaelmas, it will not bear a goose afterwards

If St Michael *(29 September)* brings many acorns,
Christmas will cover the fields with snow

## OCTOBER

Much rain in October, much wind in December

If October brings much frost and wind then January and February are mild

If the October moon appears with the points of the crescent up, the month will be dry, if down, wet

In October, dung your fields and your land its wealth will yield

If during the fall of leaves in October many leaves remain hanging and wither on the bough, a frosty winter with much snow will follow

If the hare wears a thick coat in October then lay in a good stock of fuel

October brings the acorn moon

Full moon in October without frost, no frost 'til full moon in November

A wise man carries his cloak in fair weather and a fool wants his in the rain

When the peacock loudly bawls,
Soon we'll have both rain and squalls

Bloom on the apple tree when the apples are ripe means a prompt
termination to somebody's life

When the field mouse makes its burrow with the opening to the south it
expects a severe winter, when to the north it expects rain

When the wind is in the East,
It's neither good for man nor beast,
But when the wind is in the West,
Why then it is the very best

Pluck the fruit of the rowan tree and put witches to flight

St Luke's little summer *(18 October)* - there is often a spell of fine, dry weather about this time, known as St Luke's little summer

The carrion crow creeping back again with October wind and rain

As the weather in October so it will be in March

If October brings an abundance of beech nuts, a severe winter will follow

If in October you do marry,
Love will come but riches tarry

If foxes bark much in October they're calling up a great deal of snow

Fresh October brings the pheasant
Then to gather nuts is pleasant

If the oak wears its leaves in October, you may expect a hard winter

## NOVEMBER

Mystery magnifies danger as a November fog magnifies the sun

If on All Saints' Day the beech nut be found dry, we shall have a hard winter,
But if the nut be wet and not light we may expect a wet winter

On the first of November if the weather holds clear, An end of what sowing
you do for the year

If the November goosebone *(wishbone)* be thick, so will the winter weather be

When in November the water rises, it will show itself the whole winter

November sky is chill and drear,
November leaf is red and sear

If the trees show buds in November, Winter will last until May

Ice in November brings mud in December
When the mole throws up fresh earth during a frost,
it will thaw in less than 48 hours

When rooks seem to drop in their flight as if pierced by a shot, it foreshadows rain

You can't brush a November fog away with a fan

If it is at Martinmas *(November 11)* fair, dry and cold, the cold in winter will
not last long

Where the wind is on Martinmas, there it will be through the coming winter
Severe weather at Martinmas means that the worst of the winter will be over
before Christmas

A cold November, a warm Christmas

Flowers in bloom late in the autumn indicate a bad winter

Thunder in November, a fertile year to come
As in November, so the following March

If on the trees the leaves do hold The coming winter will be cold

Flowers in bloom in late autumn indicate a bad winter

St Clements Day gives the weather for the winter

If there's ice in November that will bear a duck,
There'll be nothing after, but sludge and muck
At St Catherine's, foul or fair, so it will be next February
November take flail, let no ships sail

## DECEMBER

A green winter makes a fat churchyard

If the robin sings in the bush, then the weather will be coarse. If the robin sings in the bam, then the weather will be warm

If the Milky Way in December shows clear, you may safely count on a fruitful year

A windy Christmas is a sign of a good year

If the sun shines through the apple tree on Christmas day, there will be an abundant crop the following year

The nearer the new moon to Christmas day, the harder the winter weather

If it rain much during the twelve days after Christmas day, it will be a wet year

December 3-14, Buchan's third warm spell
A warm Christmas, a cold Easter,
A green Christmas, A white Easter

December cold with snow, good for rye

Thunder in December means fine weather

Christmas on the balcony, Easter by the fire

December takes away everything and returns nothing

Frost on the shortest day *(December 21)* is said to indicate a severe winter

If ice will bear a man before Christmas, it will not bear a mouse afterwards.

Sharp frost before Christmas means much rain afterwards

A clear and bright sun on Christmas day foretelleth a peaceable year and plenty; but if the wind grows strong before sunset it betokeneth sickness in the spring and autumn quarters
If it snows during Christmas night the crops will do well

Light Christmas, light wheatsheaf. Dark Christmas, heavy wheatsheaf

If at Christmas ice hangs on the willow, clover may be cut at Easter

If the leaves of the trees and grape vines do not fall before Martin's Day *(December 11)*, a cold winter may be expected

If the beech shows a large bud at Christmas, a moist summer will probably follow

If New Year's Eve night wind blows south, it betokeneth warmth and growth
If west, much milk and fish in the sea
If north, much cold and storms there be
If east, the trees will bear much fruit
If north-east, flee it man and brute
If the Moon if full at Christmas no blackfly will be seen on the beans.